P9-DBY-248

A Day with a Zoo Veterinarian

By James Buckley Jr.

The
Child's
World®
www.childsworld.com

Published in the United States of America by The Child's World®
1980 Lookout Drive • Mankato, MN 56003-1705
800-599-READ • www.childsworld.com

Thanks to Dr. Karl Hill and the staff at the Santa Barbara Zoo for their assistance in making this book!

ACKNOWLEDGMENTS

The Child's World®: Mary Berendes, Publishing Director

Produced by Shoreline Publishing Group LLC
President / Editorial Director: James Buckley, Jr.
Designer: Tom Carling, carlingdesign.com
Cover Art: SlimFilms
Assistant Editor: Jim Gigliotti

Photo Credits:
Cover: Mike Eliason
Interior: All pictures by Mike Eliason except: iStock 6, 7; Dreamstime.com/Kim Worrell: 19.

Copyright © 2009 by The Child's World®
All rights reserved. No part of this book may be reproduced or utilized in any form or by any means without written permission from the publisher.

LIBRARY OF CONGRESS CATALOG-IN-PUBLICATION DATA

Buckley, James, 1963–
  A day with a zoo veterinarian / by James Buckley, Jr.
     p. cm. — (Reading rocks!)
  Includes bibliographical references and index.
  ISBN 978-1-60253-098-0 (library bound : alk. paper)
 1. Zoo veterinarians—Juvenile literature. 2. Veterinary medicine—Vocational guidance—Juvenile literature. I. Title. II. Series.

 SF995.85.B83 2008
 636.089—dc22

                                        2008004389

CONTENTS

FINDING A HOME in the Zoo

The lemur has a broken leg. The Channel Islands fox needs to be fed. Two new macaws are due for their checkups, and the giraffe needs a shot. The snow leopard needs to have her teeth cleaned, too. It sounds like just another busy day in the life of a **veterinarian**!

Dr. Karl Hill is not your everyday vet, however. He doesn't just look after dogs, cats, and birds. Instead, Dr. Hill's patients all live at the Santa Barbara Zoo in California. At the zoo, he is in

Susie the Asian elephant (in the background) is Dr. Hill's biggest patient!

charge of all animal medicine. It's his job to make sure the nearly 600 animals at the zoo are healthy and happy. That's a big job, and one that takes a lot of patience and experience. But it's a job that Dr. Hill has wanted to do his whole life!

"I loved animals from the time I was very young," he says. "We had tons of pets. I tried to get even more, but my mom said no!" The Hills had cats, dogs, gerbils, guinea pigs, and a huge fish tank. Growing up in Nebraska, young Karl even had sea horses as pets.

"I knew I wanted to be a veterinarian at a zoo from the time I was a kid," Karl says. To get there, he had to study and do a lot of work.

"Vet" is a short way of saying "veterinarian."

In high school, he **volunteered** at a vet's office. "It was a great way for me to make sure that being around animals was a job I wanted to do."

People studying to be veterinarians often work with dogs and cats.

Karl went to college for four years to study **biology** and **zoology**. Then he went to veterinary school for another four years. While in college and vet school, Karl volunteered at zoos to learn more about the many different animals he would care for someday.

Dr. Hill doesn't usually feed the animals, but he had snacks for these ring-tailed lemurs today!

After finishing veterinary school, Dr. Hill worked for a while at a vet's office in Georgia. He later worked with many different animals at zoos in Atlanta, Chicago, and Texas. In 2003, his hard work paid off. He became the head veterinarian at the Santa Barbara Zoo.

An Assistant Vet

Veterinarians need help to do their job. While vets are animal doctors, veterinary technicians are like animal nurses. "Vet techs" help hold animals and keep them calm. They might give shots or wrap wounds, too. Dr. Hill's vet tech is Nancy.

At every stop along his way, Dr. Hill has learned new things about how to care for animals. He says he still learns something new all the time. "For example, I just learned how to take a blood sample from an insect," he says. "You never know when that might come in handy!"

Let's go with Dr. Hill as he visits some of his furry, feathered, and scaly friends.

2

TALKING TO THE Animals

Like a doctor who cares for people, Dr. Hill does regular checkups on his patients. **Mammals** and birds visit his office once a year. **Reptiles** and **amphibians** come by every two or three years.

The zoo has a complete medical room that includes all the machines and tools Dr. Hill needs to help his patients. This room is where animals are brought for their checkups, or if there is an emergency and they need help fast. Dr. Hill also goes out into the zoo to visit animals in their cages. You might say he gets to make "cage calls."

"I can observe the animals in their homes to make sure that medicine we gave them is working or to see if a wound is healing," he says. He and the animal keepers make sure all the animals' homes are safe.

During a checkup, Dr. Hill gives this blue and gold macaw a vitamin shot.

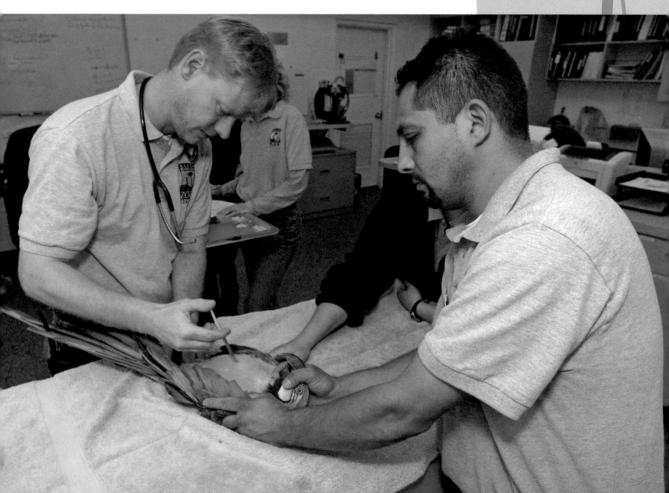

Meeting a new patient: Dr. Hill greets a meerkat as it is being moved into its new home.

Most veterinarians deal with dogs and cats, but Dr. Hill has to care for everything from anteaters to zebras. How does he do it?

"Some things are the same whether you're working with hummingbirds or elephants," he says. Those things include checking an animal's heart, breathing, eating habits, and temperature. Within each smaller group of animals, though, there are special things to look for. For example, all mammals share a few similar **traits**. "The key is to understand the differences," Dr. Hill says. "What might help one animal might hurt another animal. For example, tigers don't do well with medicine that puts them to sleep. Lions, however, deal very well with that medicine."

Don't worry, it's not dangerous! Dr. Hill and a zookeeper examine a gopher snake.

A zookeeper shows Dr. Hill how this New Caledonian giant gecko is doing.

Just like your family pets, Dr. Hill's patients have "owners." They are the zookeepers who work closely with the animals every day. Dr. Hill talks with all of them to find out how the animals are doing.

"It's a group effort," says Dr. Hill. "The keepers are my eyes and ears.

They know the animals best and are the first ones to know if there's a problem."

"Remember, animals can't tell us what's wrong. Your doctor can ask you, 'Where does it hurt?' We have to look at signs from the animal to figure out what's wrong. It's like an **investigation**."

Observing the animals himself and speaking with keepers lets Dr. Hill keep a close eye on all of his patients.

Dr. Hill observes some playful white-handed gibbons.

For more than 20 years, the Santa Barbara Zoo was home to one of the world's only giraffes with a crooked neck! Gemina was perfectly healthy, but her long neck had a sharp bend to it. Sadly, she died of old age in 2008.

Of course, some of his patients keep an eye on him, too. "I think most of the animals know me," he says with a laugh. "Many of them know me from hand-raising. That is, when they were babies, we had to help their mothers feed them. But some animals know me as the guy who comes along and hits them with a dart to put them to sleep for an exam—those animals don't like me that much!"

Dr. Hill examines most animals while they're asleep, both for his safety and for theirs. For large animals such as giraffes and elephants, he works with them while they're held safely in special **chutes**. The anteater at the zoo will eat an avocado while Dr. Hill

These giraffes get a treat while Dr. Hill checks on them.

examines her. Some birds can simply be held while they're getting checked over. Dr. Hill knows that most animals can be dangerous at times, so he's very careful when working with each and every one.

"The safety of the animals and the people working with them is our number-one concern," he says.

Some of the work Dr. Hill does is outside of the zoo. Like many zoo vets, Dr. Hill works to help the **conservation** of animals. That means helping **endangered** animals grow in numbers. Dr. Hill is an **advisor** with a program that helps snow leopards in America's zoos. He also flies to a nearby island to perform surgeries on rare Channel Islands foxes. Dr. Hill has even had to learn rock-climbing to check on California condor eggs in the rugged hills near the zoo.

"I just love that every day is different for me," he says. "I love the variety of animals and that I never know what's going to happen when I come to work!"

How do animals become endangered? It's usually our fault! People either hunt the animals or destroy the places in which they live by building cities and roads. But Dr. Hill and many others are working to help endangered animals.

One exciting part of Dr. Hill's day is giving a powerful snow leopard a checkup. Let's go behind the scenes and watch how he does it!

This California condor can be tracked by the tag on its wing.

3

SNOW LEOPARD Exam

It's checkup time for Napamar, the zoo's 16-year-old female snow leopard. She's very healthy, but just like you, she must get a checkup to make sure she's doing fine.

With a large animal like Napamar, the first step is to make her go to sleep. Dr. Hill uses a special gun to fire a small dart at her. The dart has medicine that will safely and quickly make Napamar fall asleep. Her head droops, she

Dr. Hill gets some help carrying Napamar, who weighs 80 pounds (36 kg).

yawns, and then her eyes close. Soon she's asleep, breathing softly. "Okay, let's go," Dr. Hill says. The medicine will wear off in 45 minutes, so he must work quickly. He wants to be able to check her over and give her medicines before she wakes up.

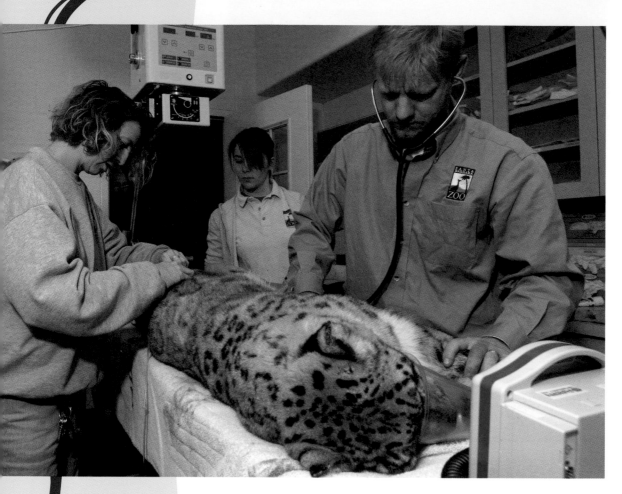

Using a stethoscope, Dr. Hill listens to the snow leopard's heart and lungs. His assistant Nancy checks Napamar's temperature.

Napamar is brought to the medical room and placed on a table. A mask is placed on Napamar's face, which will give her air and sleeping gas during the checkup. While Dr. Hill's assistant checks Napamar's temperature, he uses a **stethoscope** to listen to the snow leopard's chest. "Her lungs are clear," he calls out. An assistant keeps careful notes of the exam. Dr. Hill takes some blood samples that will be checked for diseases. He looks at Napamar's paws and claws, and even her tail.

Dr. Hill examines Napamar's paws and claws carefully, looking for cuts or wounds.

Dr. Hill feels Napamar all over, looking for any lumps or scratches that might need further checking.

As he looks in her ears with a special instrument, he sees that the top of her left ear is cut. "Our other leopard bit her there," he says. "I think we'll have to sew that up."

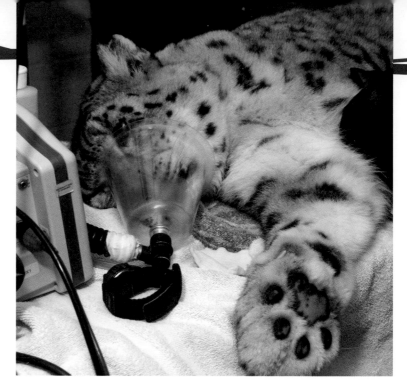

Napamar sleeps quietly during her exam. A gas mask covers her mouth and nose, giving her air and sleeping gas.

To fix Napamar's wounded ear, Dr. Hill first covers the area with blue paper that will keep the wound clean. Nancy trims the hair near the cut, and cleans the wound carefully. Dr. Hill then uses a needle, clippers, and some special thread to put several **stitches** in the ear. The stitches pull the edges of the cut together to help them heal safely and quickly. When Dr. Hill has finished, he cleans the wound again. He gives Napamar shots of medicine. After checking a few more things, Dr. Hill is almost done. But when he looks into Napamar's mouth, he doesn't like what he sees. Looks like it's time for a good teeth-cleaning! "You need to brush your teeth," he jokes to the sleeping cat. Looks like zoo vets have to be zoo dentists, too.

Fixing the cut in Napamar's ear took about seven stitches.

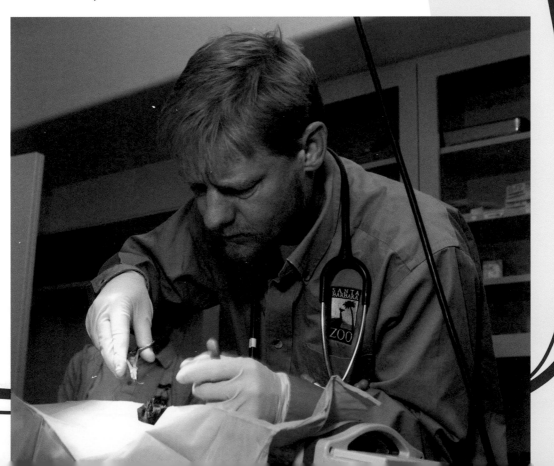

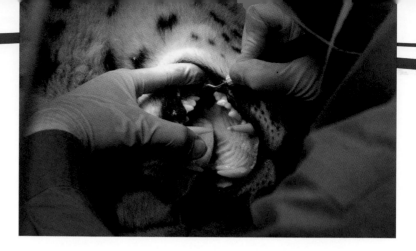

Dr. Hill scrapes Napamar's teeth to make sure she doesn't get cavities.

How do you weigh a snow leopard? Pick her up and then subtract your weight!

Before he cleans Napamar's teeth, Dr. Hill carries her to a scale to weigh her. After standing on the scale, he subtracts his weight from the number on the scale to find out how much Napamar weighs. Then he puts her on a special metal table that has a drain.

Wearing a mask and using special brushes and drills, he quickly cleans Napamar's teeth. The big cat sleeps through the whole thing.

A few minutes later, Dr. Hill pulls off his mask and checks the time—just a few minutes left before Napamar's sleeping medicine wears off!

"Okay, all done. Let's get her back quickly." Dr. Hill and an assistant carefully pick up Napamar. They carry her into her cage. After making sure she's safely inside, they watch as she slowly wakes up. In a few minutes, she's walking around after what probably felt like a nice nap.

Trimming Time

While Dr. Hill works on Napamar's teeth, two assistants clip her nails. They use a special tool to cut an inch (almost 3 cm) off her enormous claws. The claws are so thick, it takes two hands to squeeze the tool!

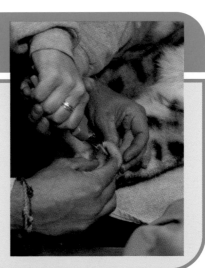

Dr. Hill has had a busy day at the zoo, but he's doing a job he loves. He had to work and study for many years, but he says it was worth it.

What if you want to become a zoo veterinarian? Dr. Hill says that being a good pet owner is a great way to start. "Watch how your pets eat and how they move. Ask a lot of questions when you take them to their veterinarian," he says.

What's the best part of his job? Dr. Hill says that he really enjoys helping a very sick or very young animal recover and have a healthy life. He tells the story of Finnegan, an endangered Channel Islands fox. Finnegan's mother was not able to

Dr. Hill checks up on one of his favorite patients, a rare Channel Islands fox named Finnegan.

care for him when he was born. For several weeks, Dr. Hill and his staff fed the tiny baby fox around the clock. "Finnegan survived and now he's doing really well. That's a story we're all very proud of."

Tomorrow is a whole new day at the zoo. Dr. Hill and his team will be there to help the animals—whether they're sick or healthy!

GLOSSARY

advisor   an expert who gives ideas on how to do things

amphibians   animals that have backbones, moist, smooth skin, and need outside heat to warm their bodies; most amphibians start out as underwater babies and change into air-breathing adults.

biology   the study of living things

chutes   narrow passages that hold large animals in place for an exam

conservation   protecting animals and plants from being harmed or wiped out altogether

endangered   having numbers so low that a plant or animal is in danger of being wiped out

investigation   a way of finding out information by studying clues

mammals   warm-blooded animals that have hair on their bodies and feed their babies milk from the mother's body

reptiles   animals that have backbones, tough skin covered with scales, and that need outside heat to warm their bodies

stethoscope   a piece of medical equipment used for listening inside a person's or an animal's body

stitches   loops of thread used to sew the edges of a wound together

traits   qualities or features

veterinarian   a doctor who treats and cares for animals

volunteered   worked without being paid

zoology   the study of animals

FIND OUT MORE

BOOKS

Gorilla Doctors: Saving Endangered Great Apes
by Patricia Turner
(Houghton Mifflin, 2005)
Go into the field with veterinarians and others working to help great apes thrive and survive.

I Want to Be a Zookeeper
by Dan Liebman
(Firefly Books, 2003)
Take a look behind the scenes of the Toronto Zoo and meet more people who work with zoo animals.

Leopards: A True Book
by Ann O. Squire
(Children's Press, 2005)
Learn about lots of types of leopards, including snow leopards like Napamar.

WEB SITES

Visit our Web site for lots of links about zoos, animals, and veterinarians: www.childsworld.com/links

Note to Parents, Teachers, and Librarians: We routinely check our Web links to make sure they're safe, active sites—so encourage your readers to check them out!

INDEX

JAMES BUCKLEY JR. has written more than 50 books for young readers on a wide variety of topics. He often takes his kids, Conor and Katie, to visit the animals at the Santa Barbara Zoo. His favorite animals there are the leaping lemurs!